Power Packed Parenting:

The Perfect Guide To Successful Parenting

Terolyn H. Fields

Power Packed Parenting

Power Packed Parenting:
The Perfect Guide to Successful Parenting

Copyright © 2017 Terolyn H. Fields

All rights reserved. No part of this publication may be reproduced or stored, in a retrieval system, or transmitted by any means, electronic, mechanical, photocopying, recording, or otherwise, without written permission from the author.

All biblical references are taken from the Amplified version of the Holy Bible unless otherwise stated.

For author appearances, inquiries and interviews contact the author by email at
www.powrpackdparenting@gmail.com

Dedication

I dedicate this book to my four amazing children – Naomi Faith, Niariah Hope, Nehemiah Agape and Noella Shalom. You have taught me so much in these past 16 years of our journey together. You didn't know it, but you provided a platform of strength for me to endure and to grow; two things I didn't always feel I had the fortitude to do, but you inspired me. I had to "make it" because I wanted to see you "make it".... And now each of you is embarking on your own journey as an adult. Don't stop learning, don't stop growing and most of all don't stop believing. I know with all my heart that each of you has what it takes to become Power Packed Parents!

Special Thanks To…

Catherine Storing – "My Writing Mama" for confirmation after confirmation after confirmation. You truly are THE Book Writing Midwife. See you on the farm!

Natalie Holloway – my divinely selected writing partner. I know there are many more books to come for both of us. Let's Do This!

Crisha Sarah Bowen – "The Giant Slayer" for helping me identify and remove those "Inner-Me-s" that were holding me back.

Louann Nealy and **Marshale Lockhart** – for believing in me and encouraging me to step out in faith!

Apostle Jonas and Pastor Rhonda Clark – for modeling and teaching me to be a Warrior of the Kingdom.

Special Thanks To...

And finally, but certainly not least...

Gladstone and Cecilia Hunter - My Parents - for teaching me, even when you didn't know you were teaching me, to become a Power Packed Parent.

Foreword

Successful parenting is a God-ordained responsibility that is essential to every child. It is a work that requires God's instruction, in order to be successful. One thing for sure, it is not "child's play".

Terolyn emphasizes several realities, which include but are not limited to, first understanding self. Her experiences and personal relationship with God have provided her with reliable tools from which parents (single and married) at any stage can draw.

Owning the responsibility to navigate the lives of children into maturity is a delicate matter, but *Power Packed Parenting: The Perfect Guide to Successful Parenting* contains valuable lessons she has learned and strategies that any parent can integrate into their journey. This book undergirds and empowers parents to accept responsibility for their decisions; for as Terolyn admonishes, children will model the decisions of their parents.

On the other hand, despite the struggles parents may face, she reminds us that children are a blessing from the Lord and she demonstrates how to embrace this honor.

Ann White, MA, MACP, RMHC
Living Water Christian Counseling

Table of Contents

Introduction 11

The Purpose Of A Parent 15

Identity Theft 25

Discipline and Correction 33

Love Versus Fear 43

Getting To The Root 49

There Are No Egos In Parenting 73

Personal Testimony 75

Pathway To Power 79

About the Author 83

Introduction

A question I'm often asked as a single parent is, "How'd you do it?" How did you raise four children by yourself? How did you come home from work and get dinner prepared after working all day? How'd you make certain each child had homework assistance when needed? How did you get to a basketball game, football game and track meet all in one week or day? How did you handle puberty, dating, sibling rivalry, spiritual development and the list goes on and on.... This is a very open-ended question, but consistently the most significant response that comes up for me when I hear this question is *"spiritual foundation"*.

Now many of us would hear that and think, "Oh yes, I take my children to church" or "Well, we don't go to church much". But the response has less to do with church and more to do with the long list of duties previously mentioned. Don't get me wrong, it is very important to provide a community of like-minded Believers for your child to develop in, but children don't necessarily learn by what they are taught as much as what is "caught" and they catch that which is modeled before them on a daily basis. Deuteronomy 6:7 speaks of us as parents walking in the light and truth of God's word ourselves first, and then teaching it to our children as we go throughout the day doing our various activities. So, the answer to the question of how to raise healthy, grounded and thriving children begins with YOU, the parent, for what is within you will come out of you – you will produce after your own kind.

The responsibility of rearing the next generation is critical to our human existence. Children must be equipped with principles like faith, discipline, perseverance, honor, integrity and other characteristics that are fundamental to the human race for future generations. There is no greater mandate on this earth than training children. It is one thing for me to coach, counsel or disciple my peers, but my children will have a longer lasting impact on society's future. Jesus said it best - ministry should first take place in Jerusalem, then in Judea, then in the uttermost parts of the earth. (Acts 1:8) I submit to you that Jerusalem is your home; Judea is your place of worship; and your workplace, friends and other spheres of influence are the uttermost parts.

Children must see consistency modeled before we can preach to them about being consistent. But this can be difficult as we are simultaneously growing on so many levels ourselves. II Corinthians 10:4-6 NKJV says:

> *... the weapons of our warfare are not carnal but mighty in God for pulling down strongholds, casting down arguments and every high thing that exalts itself against the knowledge of God, bringing every thought into captivity to the obedience of Christ, and being ready to punish all disobedience when* **your** *obedience is fulfilled. {Emphasis mine}*

With this in mind, one of the greatest challenges or hindrances that parents can have with parenting is themselves. [WAIT!! Don't shut down! Keep reading this is not a bashing session. I'm going to help you.] When we as parents are submitted and committed to walking out the principles of God's word in our own lives, we can effectively operate in the God-given authority or power we were ordained to walk in as parents, guardians and stewards.

Not only does our obedience and surrender to God give us authority in the spirit-realm, it produces the power that needs to be released when we give our children a directive and we feel confident. How do I know? Because when God ordained family, he designated a husband and wife, male and female, to train and lead children into purpose and destiny. In my home, my ex-husband was absent, totally unaccounted for in my children's lives after our marriage dissolved. So the physical presence and authority that God ordained a man to walk in was not present in my home. This authority is essential as it provides the molding and discipline that children need.

However, as a single mother it was not about trying to be "the man in the house", and no, a woman cannot teach her son "how to be a man". Moreover, I was not able to affirm my daughters' femininity and womanhood as a father would and demonstrate the strength and protection of a man. What I came to realize was that parenting is about modeling fundamental principles and characteristics in the "skin you're in", and by the grace of God, allowing His wisdom and truth to guide your parenting; whether you are single or married. Then we must trust Christ to complete the work and supply every need. Yes, this sounds easier said than done, so allow me to share more keys and strategies with you about becoming a Power Packed Parent.

The Purpose Of A Parent

Did you know you are not responsible for your child's outcome? I can hear you now, "What?!" That's right, you're not responsible for how your child turns out and this is a key revelation to becoming a successful parent. The late, great Dr. Myles Munroe said it best, "Where purpose is not known abuse is inevitable".

Unless the Lord builds the house, they labor in vain who build it... It is vain for you to rise up early, to sit up late, to eat the bread of sorrows; for he gives His beloved sleep. Behold, children are an heritage from the Lord, the fruit of the womb is a reward. Like arrows in the hand of a warrior, so are the children of one's youth. Happy is the man who has his quiver full of them. They shall not be ashamed, but shall speak with their enemies in the gate. Psalms 127:1 NKJV

I know you may be saying this sounds "super-spiritual", but it is the truth. This Psalm was the foundational scripture for me in my mid-twenties when I was married and started having children. It was an anchor and great source of strength and encouragement to me when we began building our family and people questioned or looked side-eyed at my "full quiver". With each child I held on more closely to these words embracing the inheritance that had been bestowed upon me and the weight of responsibility and stewardship I was undertaking.

Isn't it interesting how it says God is building the house; yet, parents are building the house? We all know that houses require firm foundations and the deeper the foundation, the greater the edifice's strength. If substandard work is put into the house it will be faulty and subject to collapse. The assignment of a parent is to mold, shape and nurture the gifts, God-given destiny and purpose of the child He has been blessed you with, but all too often we believe that we are fully responsible for their outcome- completely forgetting that our Father is helping us "build the house". He knows what the end looks like and advises us not to be anxious, but we have to relinquish the mindset of control and let Him assist us in the building process. It is imperative that we draw consistently from His strength and direction in order to establish that foundation.

Meditating on this passage of scripture, none of this sounds like the voluminous mental overwhelm we too often take ourselves through as parents. The caveat to all of this comes in the clause that says, *it is **vain** for you to rise up early, to sit up late, to eat the bread of sorrows; for he gives His beloved sleep.* In fact, it speaks of joy, pride and strength. When this happens, the word of God says the outcome will be rewarding. Doesn't that sound like the kind of parenting you want to experience?

This reminds me of how people often question how I "let" my daughters go "so far" away to college; one went to Massachusetts, another to Alabama while we live in Miami, Florida. Nevertheless, I was clear on what my role was as a parent. Yes, I understand that's your baby; and you carried him around for nine months; and there are crazy people out there; and the world is cruel and life is tough and, and, and… But guess what, they are going to have to deal with life just as it comes. However, if we coddle, over-protect and not allow them to fail and lovingly support them through their experiential learning, we handicap and set them up to abort the call and purpose for which their Creator designed them.

So when my oldest child was in 10th grade it was as if the Holy Spirit prompted me to start mentally preparing myself for her departure to college; and in obedience, I came into alignment with His direction. I still loved her, she would always be my "baby" (that will never change), however that was the first step- I made a decision to come into agreement when Him. I accepted it and didn't fight. This is where we struggle, not making the decision to trust His direction in simple things. When God speaks, prompts or gives us direction we must follow, regardless of how we feel. Powerful, sacrificial parenting often comes in the form of laying our lives down so that we can prove what his good, acceptable and perfect will is (Romans 12:1-2). Our feelings must be put a side so that God's glory can be manifested in our lives and His purposes fulfilled in the lives of our children.

Next we find another key point, "children are a heritage of the Lord, the fruit of the womb is a reward"! Oh my goodness! Wow! You have to let that sink in! Children are an inheritance or as defined by Merriam Webster, "something that descends to an heir". When we further explore inheritances we note that they are preserved as the original owner would have intended them to be kept or maintained. God is that original owner. He bequeaths our children to us, but He has predestined intentions for them. So in essence, our children belong to God and He has called us to be stewards. Colossians 1:16 reminds us that all things were created through Him and **for** Him.

Remember God's original mandate was to be fruitful and multiply (after His own kind) and replenish. Of course we know this is not limited to having children, but it definitely applies. Isn't it interesting also that Christ's first instruction after His resurrection is ideally the same thing. "Go ye and make disciples...." Matthew 28:19. This scripture applies to parenting as well. Discipling indicates that others are following you and your example. Each and every element of God's creation has a specified purpose, and ours as parents is to live in surrendered obedience to our Father as He grants us the grace to rear our children in the fear and admonition of Him.

This point really hit home for me when my ex-husband and children's father made the decision not to participate in their lives. Needless to say I was crushed. I was so wounded. Not only was I dealing with the dissolution of my marriage covenant and battling my own rejection, but now I had to deal with my children's abandonment and rejection as well. I could feel myself internalizing this disappointment. But one day while I was crying in my bed and sharing my pain with the Father He spoke to me and said, "I am entrusting these four lives and their destinies into your hands. I am honoring you because I can trust you". As I continued to process this, I developed a whole new perspective on my life and its current state. I no longer saw myself as an abandoned single mother of four small children, but I was being honored. I was being entrusted. In this God validated my identity as a parent. Not knowing what the end would be, not knowing what the outcome of these four lives would look like; I just knew and embraced that I had been given advanced rewards.

God has a specific plan and purpose (Jeremiah 29:11) for your child being here and He is ultimately responsible for the manifestation of that purpose coming in to fruition; and He is well able to do just that! As parents, we need to be able to discern and feel empowered to train them up into that bend. Moreover, our role is to nurture them and maintain an environment of love, which will facilitate the implementation of God's design and plan. If we do that, we can be at peace with ourselves and God that we have acted with responsible stewardship. This is all you can do, and this is all that God is asking you to do. The only other thing He is asking you to do after that is trust Him.

What beliefs have you had about what a parent is?

When you think of the ideal parent, who or what comes to mind? What has influenced this concept?

_____

_____

_____

_____

_____

When you think of ineffective parents or parenting, who or what comes to mind? What has influenced this concept?

_____

_____

_____

_____

_____

What revelation have you gained from this chapter that you can apply to your personal belief system?

_____

_____

_____

_____

_____

_____

Identity Theft

What many children lack today is an understanding of why they are here and the purpose for which they exist. This involves developing intimacy in their relationship with Christ and a desire to hear His voice and seek His direction. But again, how can we as parents lead them where we have not ourselves journeyed? Let's take this back a step. Could it be that our children are unaware because we as parents ask these same questions ourselves? It is paramount that we first understand why we are here so again let's go back to the beginning and examine the original intent of our Creator. God always provides us with a pattern; if not explicitly written out, in demonstration.

In the book of Genesis we find that God created man intentionally and gave him assignments with anticipated outcomes. He created man with fellowship in mind and they had a phenomenal relationship. What does this have to do with parenting? It has everything to do with parenting. The Father demonstrated what the primary need of our children is and that is true identity and purpose. (Genesis 1:26-28) If Adam and Eve, being the first human beings and children to exist on earth needed them, I believe a clear message is being sent that this is what we all need, parents and children alike.

The evidence is pretty clear by the chaos and confusion we see amongst our young people in the wake of a pandemic of absentee fathers, and this is not isolated to a race, as fathers can be present in the home and still "absent". Again, evidence of how important we as parents need to be clear of our own identities and purpose.

So I ask you moms and dads, are you yourself clear of your own identity and on a pathway to purpose? If you think about it, ultimately this is what we want for our children. And as the Creator did in Genesis, it is our responsibility to first make certain they develop the understanding of what their identity is and that they were designed with a specific purpose in mind.

Please know that it is ok if you don't have it all mapped out with a crystal clear plan. The point is that we and our children have a clear focus, we are on God's continued path and ever-evolving into that individual, that "authentic self" He intended us to be. As parents we set this example.

Personally, I have always been honest with my children. I have expressed that my original career path was not the ultimate platform from which the voice of my life was to speak of God's glory. I made it clear that our goal was to seek the Lord and find favor to walk through His open doors into the fulfillment of our purpose.

I grew up my entire childhood wanting to be in the medical field, but then made uninformed decisions that led me on a career path as an accountant; which hasn't been such a bad thing. However, there has always been this desire to directly care for and impact the lives of others. So I have gone through life knowing that vocationally, there was something else- something that would provide me a deeper sense of fulfillment.

So my message to my children has always been, "do whatever is in your heart to do," and the greater intimacy you have with God, the easier it will be for you to discover what He designed and created you for. Don't worry about the money. Don't worry about how many degrees you may or may not need to pursue – it won't matter because you will be walking out your passion. Your gifts will make room for you and you would be fulfilled and successful.

Does this mean that we should anticipate a detailed outline of the volumes of our lives from Him? Does He chronicle it out in a dream for some and not for others? Absolutely not, but He desires us to walk in loving fellowship with Him, as our heavenly parent while parenting our own children.

Isn't it interesting how as children proceed into their teens and into adulthood they tend to innately want to disconnect from their parent's rule? Regardless of how much they love us, innately they are really seeking a different authority. As adults, they may even still live with us, but there is this desire to pull away. Sometimes we call it rebellion and it may manifest that way. However, if we can empower our children to follow hard after their heavenly Father, this transition from parental dependence can be smoother. I believe God designed it that way, but not for teens and young adults to become wild, rebellious and out of order. Quite the opposite, as parents we equip our children to walk more independently from our nurture and care, but we should continue to model and prepare to hand them off fully under the authority of their heavenly Father and Holy Spirit. By this time they should have an understanding of how to pray and trust God to provide for their needs. They should have developed the habit of going to the House of God consistently for teaching, reinforcement of God's word and godly fellowship. Think about how the Father was there to facilitate Jesus with His purpose. Jesus would say things like, "I don't do anything except what I see My father do." The Father modeled Jesus' actions into the fulfillment of His destiny

This may all sound a little overwhelming and it feels that way sometimes. Modeling is a huge responsibility because our children are constantly watching us at every stage. Thank God for His grace because it takes the strength of His supernatural love to undergird us during difficult times. This is developed from a lifestyle of constantly relying on it, but His love is the ultimate! It can inspire and propel us to become that powerful model our children need. Let's read about it in 1 Corinthians 13:4-8

Love endures long and is patient and kind; love never is envious nor boils over with jealousy, is not boastful or vainglorious, does not display itself haughtily. It is not conceited (arrogant and inflated with pride); it is not rude (unmannerly) and does not act unbecomingly. Love (God's love in us) does not insist on its own rights or its own way, for it is no self-seeking; it is not touchy or fretful or resentful: it takes no account of the evil done to it [it pays no attention to a suffered wrong]. It does not rejoice at injustice and unrighteousness, but rejoices when right and truth prevail. Love bears up under anything and everything that comes, is ever ready to believe the best of every person, it hopes are fadeless under all circumstances, and it endure everything [without weakening]. LOVE NEVER FAILS [never fades out or becomes obsolete or come to an end]. {Emphasis mine}

As we can see from the above, love won't fail. Love endures and is patient, even when the pressure is on. It helps us get from one day to the next. But doesn't it seem, at times, that love just isn't enough? We'll talk about it as our journey continues into the next chapter.

What ideals and belief systems have you modeled as a parent about who your children are and who they are called to be? Have you been consistent?

_____

_____

_____

_____

_____

_____

Do they understand that God, the Father, is their source and has specifically designed and created them with purpose?

_____

_____

_____

_____

_____

_____

Discipline and Correction

So let's discuss discipline for a moment. As a new parent I'll never forget reading Dr. James Dobson's book <u>The Strong-Willed Child</u> and embracing a very significant, and I have found, effective nugget- we should look to discipline attitudes, not so much behaviors. This has always resonated with me. Correction is a tool that facilitates the molding and shaping of the heart. When administered correctly it should not evoke shame or guilt, but spur humility and repentance.

Being a single parent, in particular, I have had to trust God's role as Father to my children. Did He not say when a mother or father forsakes their child, He would take them up and a father to the fatherless is God (Psalm 27:10, Psalm 68:5)? Not knowing what else to do I had to stand fearlessly in God's truth and take Him at His word. So am I saying I didn't physically discipline, spank or correct my children? Not at all, because God instructs us to do so. In fact let's examine a few scriptures on discipline:

Proverbs 23:13 says:

Withhold not discipline from the child; for if you strike and punish him with the [reed-like] rod, he will not die. You shall whip him with the rod and deliver his life from Sheol (hell).

That's pretty powerful. Ephesians 6:4 says

Fathers, do not irritate and provoke your children to anger [do not exasperate them to resentment], but rear them [tenderly] in the training and discipline and the counsel and the admonition of the Lord.

So I know the next question is, "How should I correct?" Well, firstly, correction should be age appropriate and purpose-driven. Don't correct, **just because** you are angry or simply because your child has done something you do not like. Okay, let's talk about the types of correction. Of course the big inquiry is spanking. Yes, I believe in spanking. It is biblical. Foolishness (or folly) is bound in the heart of a child, but the rod of correction shall drive it far from him. (Proverbs 22:15) But what I found was if done appropriately, it rarely has to be used. Young children do not always understand the rationale behind the direction being given them. Remember, most often, correction is about protection. So in the case of the 2 year old that wants to stick an object in the electrical socket, how strong of a message do you think a "time out" will give? That might require a different method of correction. Not lashing them with many stripes, but taps on the hands with a ruler or paddle (because hands are for loving and hugging only) and a strong "No". Now you're establishing your God-ordained authority; they must listen to you; and that particular action has detrimental consequences. For the child, they equate the socket with the unpleasant taps, but you know the ultimate consequence could be death.

Now if a child spills a glass of milk, that doesn't warrant a spanking. They need direction at that point, "Don't play with your toy at the dinner table". However, if the child disregards, your direction, brushes you off and continues to play with the ball that warrants a spanking. Why? Because that is rebellion manifesting, which is an attitude or position of the heart that says, "I'm choosing not to listen to you". Rebellion is a characteristic trait that if continually practiced, has detrimental consequences. In other words, if rebellion is not dealt with at the age of three while playing at the dinner table, it shows up at thirteen as not coming home directly after school as instructed or stealing, etc., etc. What's most important is consistency and patience. This again is where many of us as parents need prayerful strength. We have to be consistent from incident to incident and from child to child. We cannot discipline an issue one day and let it slide the next. We can't correct a behavior with one child and let another get away with it.

In addition to spanking I believe clear and open communication is imperative. Don't just spank your child and walk off. After both of you have had a moment to cool off and process the situation, it is very important to come back and discuss with your child why you have taken the action that you have. In the instance of not coming home on time, explain the implications of wandering around in the streets alone with friends. Use examples from the media of the results of that behavior (child trafficking for example).
I remember when my daughter had just entered high school and asked me to go with her friends to a pool

party at the home of a celebrity. We went back and forth a few times until finally I said – wait a minute, I can show you better than I can tell you. All of a sudden, the Spirit of God gave me an idea. I went to YouTube and showed her footage of entertainer-pool parties that had gotten out of control. Needless to say, the pool party wasn't so important any more.

However, hear your child out. Be sensitive to their perspective. In their minds they have a valid reason for doing what they do. Listening to them with an open heart will open the doors for mutual respect. Maybe a primary reason for a child lingering late afterschool is that they're hungry and going to the corner store to get a snack. Solution: buy some extra snacks from the store that your child can take to eat on the way home – problem solved. Maybe they just want to spend time with their friends. This is where we have to exercise patience and be creative- offer a monthly outing with friends in exchange for punctuality. The point is sometimes as parents we just want our own way, and have to allow God to stretch us in the area of patience (more on that later). Our goal is to train our children on how to make sound decisions. This can't be accomplished with just a flat, "No" all the time.

Keeping the lines of communication open is vital, a thread that should be woven throughout the duration of your relationship. This CAN be achieved without compromising your authority or trying to transform into a "senior teenager" (smile).

The biggest mistake we can make as parents when disciplining, particularly when it comes to spanking, is disciplining out of emotion. It's the times when we are so angry that "Johnny" got in the fight at school and embarrassed the household name- "Susie" used her baby food for hair conditioner and now we have to laboriously shampoo it out or Michelle was caught kissing in the stairwell- that we forget the purpose of discipline is for behavioral correction. It's ultimately about correction, not making them pay for what they have done or exacting vengeance. It is not a time to release all of the frustration of the workplace or personal battles. At times like this, both parent and child need a "time out" and then we can revisit the disciplining process. The situation will still be there.

We were never designed to function outside of the power, love and wisdom of the Father, but we often walk around from day to day laden with fears, produced from lies, that we have rehearsed; and it comes out in our parenting. In the next chapter we will examine how the purity of our love can get over-shadowed even when our only desire is to do what's best for our children.

How do you define discipline and what is its purpose?

_____

_____

_____

_____

_____

_____

_____

_____

_____

_____

_____

How do you "show up" during times of discipline and correction?

_____

_____

_____

_____

_____

Is this working for you? Has it been reliable?

_____

_____

_____

_____

_____

What is the distinction between discipline and abuse?

_____

_____

_____

_____

_____

_____

How has this chapter changed your perspective around discipline and correction?

_____

_____

_____

_____

_____

_____

Love Versus Fear

For God did not given us a spirit of timidity (of cowardice, of craven and cringing and fawning fear), but [He has given us a spirit] of power of love and of calm and well-balanced mind and discipline and self-control. 2 Timothy 1:7

In everything we do, we must remember that we are created in the image and likeness of our Daddy, and hence should do as He does. Oh! What a beautiful model of parenting He provides! So who is God and how does He successfully parent? The Bible tells us that God is Love (1 John 4) and so, that's how He parents through love. I know by now you must be saying, "But I do love my kids", and I am not arguing or taking that from you; but let's consider this, could that love be diluted and/or impotent because of fear? At this point you may or may not be able to answer that. [Just stay with me, we're going somewhere.] However, everything that God calls us to do; He calls us to do from a place of love. Whether we are just dialoging with our child, playing or reading, correcting and/or disciplining, all must be done from a place of love. On the other hand, what often shows up is fear, in some form, instead. How does fear show up in parenting? It shows up as either an "Authoritarian Parent" or a "Permissive Parent", both of which are rooted in fear.

Examples of these look like this: The stay-at-home mom of a toddler that is ruling the entire house-hold (even the cat) when dad leaves for work. The father who is haunted daily and petrified to see his baby-girl grow up and possibly lose her virginity so he never lets her out of the house? Whatever our station or status we **must not** let fear overwhelm or drive us.

One thing that can make parenting difficult is that our decisions are made from a tapestry of influences. Hence, it is so important to know where we are, where we stand and what's going on with ourselves before we judge or try to figure out what's going on with our children. Everything we do and all of the decisions we make are filtered through our personal, and sometimes skewed, perspectives. This is why we started the conversation of this book out by gaining clarity on what God's, the Creator of Family, perspective is on parenting.

I have often felt criticized for not being "hard enough" in certain instances. This has elicited pressure at times to "lay down the law", in an attempt to force something to happen with my children. But the Holy Spirit has often come and settled me during those times and caused me to realize that I am not in a battle for control. I have authority. There is no power struggle here, and I am not going to engage in that level of warfare. It is in that moment that I have learned to take a step back, breathe and prayerfully surrender that situation to Him. I seek His direction, because that is who I am ultimately accountable to. That's the big picture, not how well I throw my weight around, but how fearlessly obedient I am to the voice of the Lord. This is done by walking in a loving relationship with the Father.

Have you ever tried declaring God's word or affirmations over your life and the life of your children, but the words just seemed empty and vain? You felt like you were struggling to believe what you're even saying. This is a clear indication that there is a problem with your own belief system. And, where there is a problem with belief, there is doubt and doubt is rooted in fear. Fear can be an intrinsic weapon against all that we desire and God wants for our lives. It is a false thought process, altered reality or just a plain lie that inhibits us from believing and releasing the spoken word and truth with conviction and power. What's worse is that it diminishes our confidence and authority; authority in every area of our lives, including parenting.

Recognizing these areas of fear and impotence requires transparency with our selves. Fear shows up in so many ways, but assuredly if you sense that you are emotionally "charged" in a negative way, fear is probably at the root of it.

Fear manifests as being overly permissive because of our own previous rejections. It manifests as control and impatience from our own experiences of abuse. It shows up as shame-based disciplining, because we carry our own insecurities. How about this, does your marriage lack the intimacy it should and you've become hyper-focus on your child, spoiling your child (and further distancing yourself from your spouse or partner)? Or maybe you just feel the pressure to have a "perfect" family, like the one you think you grew up in. These are all examples of behavior that cloak fear. For this reason, in the next chapter we will explore some of the doorways through which fear enters our lives, attempts to take up residence and disempowers us from walking in the fullness of our God-ordained power and authority as parents.

Would you say you are more of an authoritarian or permissive parent? What characteristics or examples lend you to describe yourself this way?

_____

_____

_____

_____

_____

Do you know what factor(s) have influenced you to operate this way?

_____

_____

_____

_____

_____

Getting To The Root

Do you sometimes feel "out of control as a parent"? Ever feel like you can't get your children to respond and do what you want them to do? Do you ever feel guilty about the behaviors you see in them; like it's your fault that they are the way they are? In this chapter we will explore why we sometimes experience these feelings, bring comfort and clarity; and empower you to stop feeling this way.

As we previously stated fear brings torment and self-fulfilling prophecy. Job said it best,

For the thing which I greatly fear comes upon me, and that of which I am afraid befalls me. Job 3:25

Fear and love can't coexist. All too often we are afraid and don't even know it because we've lived with these fears for so long. As parents, we love our children, but sometimes that love is suffocated and we are inhibited from parenting from a place of power, love and soundness of mind.

One key that is paramount to successful parenting is that it occurs in the spiritual as well as natural realm. There are many spiritual principles that we innately follow, like giving our children wise instruction – who told us to do that? Or what about when you just "know" when your child is not being truthful. It's as if there is a supernatural instinct that directs us to know, and do certain things. On the other hand, it is difficult to operate from this place of supernatural power and receive daily direction from the Holy Spirit when our own spirits are bound and our emotions are inflamed with various issues and fears. God's reality for us is that we are led by His Spirit in every area of our lives, including parenting.

Our souls (mind, will and emotions) will flag us and tell us that something is going on with us. What's driving you? What is leading your parenting decisions? Sometimes we tend to think that we should respond carefully with everyone else in our lives, except those in our own households, especially our children. Whenever we sense that our emotions (discouragement, rejection, anger) are really sensitive and taking over, we must pause and see what's going on.

The following are essential areas that we should explore and inventory within our lives in order to discover our triggers. These themes create fear and emotional charges that inhibit us from walking in that place of power that we want to walk in as parents. These areas adversely affect our belief system; dilute our love and obedience to the voice of God.

Generational Curses

Simply put, generational curses are areas, belief systems or behaviors that we see repeatedly manifest within our families. They are repeated cycles from one generation to the next. Perhaps back in our bloodline a relative opened a door to abuse, sexual promiscuity (of all kinds fornication, adultery, homosexuality), substance abuse, sickness and the list goes on and on. "Familiar Spirits" are now assigned to the family to test and tempt the family members. They look for signs of agreement with that behavior, **binding** family members to such behaviors or patterns for decades and even centuries.

Of course, as we identify obvious self-destructive behaviors, we should make every effort to get assistance and stand for our deliverance. Note that there will be a fight, but the Father's delivering ability is real! On the other hand, what about the less obvious curses that are passed down – like patterns of thinking and thought processes? Sometimes there are parenting traits or characteristics that can be passed down as well. Belief systems that limit your child's growth and fulfillment of God's best plan for their lives should be challenged and questioned. **Remember, that is our ultimate assignment.** An example of this is, no one in your family has ever attended college because it was always **believed** that it was too expensive and you now have inhibitions about your child going for these same reasons. Nevertheless, your child has a strong passion to pursue some professional career path. If the Father has predestined that child to become an attorney and be a righteous voice against injustice, He will make provision for it to happen.

Can you see how a generational curse of poverty thinking can limit and hinder the plan of God for your child's life? We cannot allow distorted beliefs that have been passed down to become stumbling blocks to our children's destinies. Perhaps it's a parenting trait of thinking that it's okay to call a child out his name because your mother did it to you. What parenting DNA are you carrying or should be examined? Yes, it will be uncomfortable to dismantle, but remember you are doing it in the name of love and renouncing improper, familiar beliefs to align with God's truth and it will give you greater authority in prayer to deal with your child's issues. Here's the key:

For though we walk in the flesh, we do not war according to the flesh. For the weapons of our warfare are not carnal but mighty in God for pulling down strongholds, casting down arguments and every high thing that exalts itself against the knowledge of God, bringing every thought into captivity to the obedience of Christ, **and being ready to punish all disobedience when your obedience is fulfilled.** *2 Corinthians 10:3-6*

In other words, we cannot overcome in an area with our children, until we gain victory over ourselves. And often, the very thing that bothers us or we clash about with them needs to be dealt with first within us.

Past Disappointments-Molding Them Into Your Own Image

Make peace with your past. Don't parent solely from your own perspective. Often parents live vicariously or subconsciously through their children, from an adverse perspective. For example, (does this sound familiar) a father who disrespected women in his youth, is overprotective of his teenage daughter who is trustworthy and has not given him reason not to be trusted. Or what about the mother that didn't get to fulfill some of the dreams she wanted to and now intensely drives her child (because of fear) towards perfection and some "unknown goal". It is very important that we do not try to mold our children **into our own images and likenesses.** Each individual that God puts on this earth has his own personality, bend and purpose. It's our responsibility to help our children discover their own God-given uniqueness gifts and interests. We should not try to make them fit into a mold we have constructed. I have even found that areas of gridlock between me and my children are sometimes just simple personality differences.

On another note, it is not our responsibility to define what success looks like for our children. If we **model** what "success" looks like, consistently practicing the word of God and the values that we expect of them, we can more than likely be assured that they will follow. Two keys here: Are we modeling and truly practicing what we preach? Can they see the results of what we have taught them manifesting in our own lives? If we have done that then we can be confident that we have done ALL that the Father has asked us to do. However, perhaps we have not always consistently modeled as we should. (And let's be clear here, I'm not talking behavioral perfection, but an unfailing surrender and pursuit to please the Father.) Not to fear, because God is greater and able to reconcile our weaknesses when we repent and change our ways. Guilt is another form of fear that keeps us paralyzed and stuck from doing what is right. Look at this:

Whenever our hearts in [tormenting] self-accusation make us feel guilty and condemn us. [For we are in God's hands] For He is above and greater than our consciences (our hearts), and He knows (perceives and understands) everything [nothing is hidden from Him]. 1 John 3:20

Undoubtedly, will they test the waters and step outside of the boundaries that we have established or provided? Probably, but at that point, this is where we are expected to trust the mighty hand of our Father to lead, guide and yes, correct them, just as he has done with us. Yes, I know that is challenging and no, my intent is not to be cavalier, but this is where we have to really check ourselves and determine how much we are trusting the Father, with His "inheritance". Give yourself a break, when you can say with full assurance you've done your part, trust God to do His. Sometimes we let the scripture below become too familiar. Instead, we can anchor ourselves in the trust that His desires for success are far greater than our own.

Train up a child in the way he should go [and in keeping with his individual gift or bent], and when he is old he will not depart from it. Proverbs 22:6

I remind God, "You said 'they would not depart'", so although I may see actions that don't line up with the "way that they should go" I trust the Father to get them on track, just as He has done over and over in my own life. Let God be God in your child's life. They need their own testimony.

Past Hurts and Wounds

I'm sure you've heard it before: Hurting people hurt people, rejected people reject people…

It is impossible to love anyone when our own hearts are not freed to receive love. True, pure Love is not about an emotion. Emotions occur in our mind or soul-realm and there is nothing wrong with them, outside of the fact that they need to be surrender to the Spirit of God. Love is a spiritual entity. God is love. If we have not allowed the Word and blood of Jesus to heal and deliver us from hurts, rejections and abuses, the presence and love of God will not freely flow in and through us to anyone, particularly our children. Mind you, this can be a process, depending on how deep our emotional wounds are.

Often what we "feel" as love is infatuation, lust or a deep satisfaction of our own unmet emotional needs. None of this is love. Love is a moment by moment decision to honor, respect and walk out the characteristics previously discussed in 1 Corinthians 13 (in the *Love Versus Fear* chapter) and yes, that goes for children too. There is a certain amount of plain old human respect that children are entitled to. Just because we may be carrying around a load of pain and frustration, doesn't give us the right to negligently or abusively mishandle them. No matter what they have done.

Remember children are our inheritance, something to be prized and cherished. If we are not equipped to treat them in that manner, then we must make a decision to get the help and deliverance we need to position ourselves for parenting success. Awareness and acknowledgement are the greatest steps, and then comes the decision. Everything starts with a decision. Once we firmly decide to deal with our own hurts and wounds (if for no other reason than the love we have for them) the ability and resources we need will become available. Be resolute about pursuing the healing you need so you don't transfer your hurts and wounds to your child.

Successful parenting establishes a foundation of nurturing and exemplifies the character of Father God, who is our ultimate parenting model. Do you know His love? Have you allowed yourself to come into intimate relationship with Him and let Him heal your brokenness and pain? After my divorce I knew I had to do this. I never wanted to be full of pain and bitterness. I had to let go of my pain (repeatedly) and say, "Lord, I give it to You. You bore wounds on your back so I would not have to carry my own, here take it". And He agreed to take it, but the next thing I had to do was decide to forgive.

Unforgiveness

Unforgiveness is a literal cancer, like a disease that eats away from the very breath of life within us. Moreover it is a profound dissolver of love, not just towards the individual we hold hostage, but to the love we have for everyone including God.

But if you do not forgive, neither will your Father in heaven forgive your failings and shortcomings. Mark 11:26

This was the scripture that delivered me from battling with unforgiveness. Unforgiveness is such a deceiver. While you feel you are exacting vengeance on your offender you are actually binding yourself up and giving someone else control in your life and the life of your child. How? Because everything you mentally process is filtered through that unforgiveness and can make your love "conditional", whether you realize it or not. Love, particularly toward our children, should not have conditions based on what someone else has done. A key area that can trip you up as parents is unforgiveness towards your own parents. Often as we mature, and come into our own adulthood we are able identify the weaknesses and even mistakes of our parents. But who are we to judge? Matthew 7:1-2 says:

Do not judge and criticize and condemn {your parents}, so that you may not be judged and criticized and condemned yourselves. For just as you judge and criticize and condemn {your parents} you will be judged and criticized and condemned, and in accordance with the measure you (use to) deal out to {your parents}, it will be dealt out again to you. Why do you stare from without at the very small particle that is in {your parents'} eye but do not become aware of and consider the beam of timber that is in your own eye? {Insertions mine}

How often do we as adults carry unforgiveness towards our parents and then end up living out the very thing we detest in them. Judgment causes blind-spots and inhibits us from being able to see ourselves as we really are. For example, I watched someone walk blindly in their father's footsteps, after judging his absenteeism from their life. This person heavily criticized their father and NEVER had anything positive or compassionate to say about him. They later found out that their mother, in her desire to protect them from their father's abuse, discouraged their father's presence in their life. I'm sure if he had known better, he would have done better; but just did have done better but didn't know how. Consequently, what has manifested? This person became abusive and abandoned his own children. At the root of unforgiveness is bitterness and anger, and at the root of every anger is really a fear – some fear due to lack of control. Think about it…

And most importantly, forgive yourself. Forgive yourself for the decisions you've made that may not have produced optimal, comfortable or wrong results.

At the end of the day, that's what it boils down to; decisions that just didn't provide the intended expectation. Release the guilt. Let go of the shame. As parents we do the best that we know to do given the environment we've come from and the behaviors we've seen modeled or learned for coping with life's issues. But we do have the power and can be empowered as parents when we walk in forgiveness. This is why is it vitally important for us to discover what emotionally charges or influences our actions so that we can pass on a healthy parenting legacy to our children.

Lack of Patience

I believe it goes without saying that every parent is tried and tested in the area of patience. However, it is important to recognize that this is an area that we MUST not only be tested in, but also be willing to grow in. (I would say "master", but I don't think we ever feel as though we can "master" patience. There will always be another test. Patience is a virtue where we must learn to surrender our will and trust. Let's face it, any and every time our children don't do what we ask, instruct, or expect our patience is challenged. This is an organic characteristic of our human nature. We all want control. The key thing to note about parenting, however, is that it is more about authority than it is control.

Have you ever realized how much in life we really don't have control of? Ever been laid off from a job, suffered an accident, gone through a health issue or crisis – these are all life issues that test or strengthen our patience. As we go through it, one day we finally get to the place where we stop fighting the circumstance and realize we don't have complete control. Yes, we can do things to mitigate the brunt, implement structure and processes to facilitate the progress of the occurrence; but at the end of the day we can't wave that magic wand and make it happen. We can, however, walk in authority – authority is the key. Let's look at the Merriam Webster definition of authority: *the power to influence or command thought, opinion or behavior.* Isn't this how God deals with us? He presents truth, encourages, chastens and is very patient. He didn't even snatch the fruit out of Adam and Eve's hands! (I told you He's the best parenting model!)

As a parent, we have God-ordained authority and when we are surrendered and trust Him, He has our back. He knows how to turn the heart of our children and He will back and confirm our words. Now don't get me wrong, when we give our children a repeated command not to run out in the street, there should be an immediate obedience, followed by spanking at the indication that they want to rebel and not comply.

However, as our children grow, our goal should be to have established a love, trust and respect that cause us to have great influence with them. After all, we want our child to grow up and be able to make sound decisions independently. Of course they will come to us (and others) for sound counsel, but our egos should not be so caught in the way that we get offended or hold grudges when they don't "do as we say" as they become adults. The intention is not to get into power struggles with toddlers and small children. Be firm, be consistent – don't worry about whether they like you or not because you told them to stop throwing their Jell-O across the room. Make certain that your objective is the end result. Do not turn the situation into a battle of wills. This is the manifestation of fear. It demonstrates that you are not walking in the authority you have been given? I can hear it, "Suppose I don't get my way?" The goal is not to get "your way", but to either 1) teach your child something or 2) achieve some end result.

How often has something simple turned in to a battle of wills? If it's not an immediate matter of life or death, take a step back from the situation and allow the Holy Spirit to give you wisdom and a strategy concerning the matter. He will do it. Sometimes it's just a matter of allowing the situation a moment to diffuse and giving Him an opportunity to bring the conviction that only He can bring. Make sure your ego or impatience doesn't get in the way and sabotage the influence or overall relationship.

I had a great victory in this area when one of my daughters began dating. I could see she was being torn down and disrespected. She was away in college and when she would come home I could observed she was morphing into someone else. Because of our distance, I was not able to implement any direct boundaries or consequences to influence her on an on-going basis. I had NO control, but I had authority. First, I prayerfully asked the Lord to cover and protect her from any abuses (emotional or physical) and to open the eyes of her understanding. I had NO control, but deep in my heart I knew God wanted better for her so We were in agreement. I'd talk to her from time to time about how I felt, but she continued in the relationship. Yet I was still confident that God would faithfully allow her to see the truth. I remained focused on what I knew the Father could do, and didn't bash or insult her when we spoke. God strategically used other friends and mentors to periodically speak the same truth to her and at the appointed time she was through with the relationship – it just took patience!

We hear it all the time, "a little patience goes a long way". Often we lack patience because we think the current situation we are encountering will resolve whatever internal conflicts or emotional charges we are experiencing. It could further appear we are giving that person or circumstance permission to control us. In actuality, if we would step back, not rush to get our own way; get clear and acquire our own internal peace; find out the root and reason behind what is really bothering us; we will be more empowered and hear God's creative strategies for resolving issues with our children. "Time out" can be a good thing for both child and parent.

What generational curses (repeated behaviors of defeat) do you see in your family?

_____

_____

_____

_____

_____

What improper parenting beliefs do you think you may have inherited?

_____

_____

_____

_____

_____

What fear(s) resides in your heart? What is tucked away so deep, the source of which is forgotten on a conscious level but rules and reigns in your life from a subconscious level?

_____

_____

_____

_____

_____

Is there a hurt or disappointment that you repeatedly talk about although it occurred years ago?

_____

_____

_____

_____

_____

Are you still disappointed with your parents about or something(s) they did or didn't do; or said to you? Have you forgiven them?

_____

_____

_____

_____

_____

_____

Do you look to control situations with your children or the routine of their lives?

_____

_____

_____

_____

_____

_____

Are you willing to trust God to show your children the way and give them direction? Can you think of a specific area in which you need to do this?

_____

_____

_____

_____

_____

What steps can you take to get free from the bondages that you have discovered during the journey of reading this book?

_____

_____

_____

_____

_____

Are you willing to take these steps in order to be healthy, successful parent?

_____

_____

_____

_____

_____

_____

There Are No Egos In Parenting

There is godly wisdom and there is the wisdom of man. Godly wisdom supersedes the wisdom of man EVERYTIME. Let me say it this way, the Bible says in the multitude of counsel there is safety, so yes, seek counsel, but do not allow the carnal voices in your life to drown out the voice of godly wisdom.

Ask God- He has the answers. He has solutions. He will work with you when you are submitted to His direction. Moreover, you will be able to walk in greater confidence because your *faith is not resting in the wisdom of men, {human philosophy}, but in the power of God. 1 Corinthians 2:5 {Insertion mine}* Know that the Father honors those that honor Him. He'll give you so much favor and reverence in the sight of your children when you allow Him to have authority in your life.

Most importantly, none of the results from wisdom or strategies in this book, or any other will manifest overnight. This is why humility and patience, which was discussed in the previous chapter, are so vitally important. Everything in life has some form of process. Whether building a house or building our children, we have to implement the instructions given and allow them to settle. We have to be flexible and willing to first pursue growth within ourselves. All too often as people of God, we function from one of two extremes. We are either so "super-spiritual", until we are barely any earthly good or full of sensuality, perceiving only from our senses. We must learn how to navigate between the two. This is done by abiding in the presence of God and allowing the power of His love to reign and have preeminence. It is then that we are empowered to parent successfully.

Personal Testimony

The answer to "How'd You Do It" is: I personally decide to be a surrendered, spirit-filled Believer and grow in the grace of Jesus Christ and follow the voice of His Spirit. This is not a one day instantaneous occurrence, but a life-long commitment and process. And although I read many parenting books about breast-feeding, discipline, and parenting a strong-willed child, nothing pales in comparison to the direction I receive from day to day. The weapons of my parenting warfare are not just natural, but I position myself to utilize spiritual weapons and never stop growing in the art of spiritual war. I stay on the offense- knowing what kind of climate my children started out in. There was arguing, emotional and mental abuse and a lot of fear. So a couple of my favorite declarations have been these:

My children shall be taught of the Lord and great shall be their peace; Isaiah 54:13

My children are His sheep and know His voice and the voice of another (rejection and abandonment) they will not follow. John 10:5

You have to have scriptures and words of affirmation to which you can anchor your faith. Faith has to have a target.

One thing I have learned during this parenting journey and that is to look at myself first. When I am clear, my heart is clean and I am aligned with the Father's heart and mind He is able to do what I can't. Let me give you a quick example:

Recently, my daughter's iPhone 5 started malfunctioning so I resolved that it was time to purchase a new one. Later she came to me and began a campaign for the new iPhone 8. "Absolutely not!" Was my thought, but hey, I'm a parent and I know my kid, she's persistent. So the waltz ensued, I said "no", a 7plus was sufficient. I continued my stance of "no" as I could see no practical reason. She claimed the IPhone 8 was a better phone. Finally, I just put my foot down, having allowed her the opportunity to respectfully express herself and her desires; but I let her know that it just wasn't going to happen. I was paying for it and that was the end of it. For the next day or so, the air was a little tight between us – she wanted the phone and I was irate because I had been challenged.

But why was I still so irate? I mean I was livid, but couldn't understand why over such a minor issue. So I went to the Father with an open heart seeking understanding about my OWN attitude first and this was His response: "What about the times that I ask you to do something and you go back and forth with me?" **BAM**! All of a sudden all the frustration I had been experiencing instantaneously and literally seemed to melt. Needless to say, the next time I saw my daughter, her attitude had shifted as well. The next day we went and purchased her 7 plus – another victory for parent and child!

Pathway To Power

During this journey you may have discovered or uncovered some areas or obstacles that may feel difficult to face and overcome on your own. I pray that this book has motivated you to become "your best self" so that you can feel confident and empowered as a parent, but liberated to walk in authority in every area of your life. We must be aware of the barriers that inhibit us from walking in the love and power that God has ordained for us, in order to be good stewards of the children He has blessed us with. **Know that you are not alone and** that there is no condemnation in Christ. (Romans 8:1)

Each and every one of us has to deal with these life issues; the key is not to ignore them, but doing what it takes to get free and cooperating with the Holy Spirit's wisdom. It all starts with a decision. All change starts with a decision. If you are not satisfied with the results you are seeing in your kids, if you're seeing repeated conflict in a certain area or find that you are constantly emotionally charged about something, prayerfully check yourself first. And I'm not talking about a one minute prayer. I mean humbly and fervently seek the Lord and He will give you the answers you need. Quietly, meditate and allow Him to bring you into a space of light and truth. Make up in your mind to look those generational curses, familiar spirits, hurts, wounds and unforgiveness in the face and overcome them. It is possible. That is where our victory lies and our ability to become Power Packed Parents!

If you feel that this pathway will be too difficult for you to travel alone, I encourage you to seek professional assistance or just someone to partner with you - start with a mentor, coach or the counsel of your spiritual leadership.

Certified professional life coaching services are just an email away and can help you work through blockages and set goals for yourself to shift into a more confident, healthier place.

Contact me at powrpackdparenting@gmail.com or visit my website: www.powrpackdparenting.com for more information.

{FREE BONUS OFFER}

Join me for a virtual Master Class in January 2018 to discuss more insights and strategies about becoming a Power Packed Parent!

Register here: www.powrpackdparenting.com

About the Author

Terolyn Naomi Hunter Fields received Christ as her Lord and personal savior at the age of 11. This monumental decision occurred through the prompting of the Holy Ghost, after a sermon entitled "You Need God In Everything You Do".

She grew up as many young people do - "walking to the beat of their own drum' - until her final semester at Florida A&M University when she decided to rededicate her life to Christ. It was at this time that she realized how much she really needed God in everything she did, and that has remained true to this day.

Terolyn is a divorcee and single parent of four amazing children who are her pride and joy. Although her hands have been full parenting her own children for the past 16 years, she has become affectionately known as "Mama T" to a group of young women she began mentoring in 2005 known as "Virtuous Vessels".

Being a natural leader, leadership has never been foreign to her, as she holds strong values around empowering and encouraging growth in others. Although she has held numerous such roles in her professional accounting career, she finds her greatest fulfillment and purpose as a conference speaker and professional life coach; which has led to her latest project, the authoring of her first book, <u>Power Packed Parenting: The Perfect Guide To Successful Parenting.</u>

Made in the USA
Columbia, SC
30 May 2025